SPORTS CLINIC

Football:
Rushing
and
Tackling

By Stephen Holden

HIGH
interest
books

Children's Press
A Division of Grolier Publishing
New York / London / Hong Kong / Sydney
Danbury, Connecticut

This book is dedicated to my friend and fellow football fan, Darrell Davis.

A special thanks to Roselle High School in Roselle, New Jersey

Book Design: Nelson Sa
Contributing Editor: Rob Kirkpatrick

Photo Credits: Cover © Angelo Barros and Nelson Sa; p. 5 © Brian Bahr/All Sport; p. 6 © Jamie Squire/All Sport; p. 8 © Andy Lyons/All Sport; pp. 11, 13 © Angelo Barros and Nelson Sa; p. 14 © Todd Warshaw/All Sport; p. 17 © Andt Lyons/All Sport; p. 18 © Jamie Squire/All Sport; pp. 20, 22, 24 © Angelo Barros and Nelson Sa; p. 27 © Todd Warshaw/All Sport; p. 28 © Al Bello/All Sport; pp. 30, 32 © Angelo Barros and Nelson Sa; p. 35 © Doug Pensinger /All Sport; p. 36 © Jamie Squire/All Sport.

Visit Children's Press on the Internet at:
http://publishing.grolier.com

Library of Congress Cataloging-in-Publication Data

Holden, Stephen, 1969-
    Football : rushing and tackling / by Stephen Holden.
    p. cm. – (Sports clinic)
    Includes bibliographical references and index.
    ISBN 0-516-23365-3 (lib. bdg.) – ISBN 0-516-23565-6 (pbk.)
    1. Football—Defense—Juvenile literature. [1. Football.] I. Title. II. Series.

GV951.18.H64 2000
796.332'26—dc21

    00-028265

CONTENTS

INTRODUCTION

Time is running out in Super Bowl XXXIV. The St. Louis Rams have a 23-16 lead, but the Tennessee Titans are coming back. They have the ball on the Rams' ten-yard line, but they only have time for one more play.

The Titans snap the ball. Quarterback Steve McNair drops back and looks for an open receiver. He throws the ball to wide receiver Kevin Dyson. Dyson catches a short pass and turns toward the St. Louis end zone. It looks like Dyson is going to score a touchdown and tie the game!

But wait! Rams linebacker Mike Jones steps up and hits Dyson. He wrestles Dyson to the ground. As he is tackled, Dyson reaches toward the end zone with the ball. Dyson hits the ground. The football is in his hand, on the one-yard line. Time runs out. The Rams win! They are the Super Bowl champs—by the margin of one yard!

The St. Louis Rams defense made a big play to win Super Bowl XXXIV.

4

There's a saying in football: defense wins championships. The teams in Super Bowl XXXIV had a lot of great offensive players. But in the end, a defender made the biggest play of the game. This book teaches the keys to playing defense. In the game of football, this comes down to two things: tackling the ball carrier and rushing the quarterback.

DEFENSIVE POSITIONS

During running plays, the defense's first goal is to tackle the player carrying the ball. During passing plays, the defense's first goal is to stop the quarterback from making the pass. This is called rushing the passer.

Each defensive player has his own position. Each position has different responsibilities. By covering their positions, defenders give themselves the best chance to stop whatever the defense throws at them.

DEFENSIVE LINEMEN

Teams line up with either three or four defensive players on the line of scrimmage. There are two types of defensive linemen: defensive tackles and defensive ends. Sometimes, a defense uses three linemen: one tackle and two ends.

Defensive linemen try to stop the ball carrier at or behind the line of scrimmage.

Defensive Positions

Defensive linemen have to be big and strong. The offensive linemen try to block the defensive linemen. The defensive linemen need to get past these blocks. They also need to tackle ball carriers.

Defensive Tackle

A defensive tackle lines up in the middle of the defensive line. In a three-man defensive line, or front, the tackle lines up directly in front of the offensive center. This tackle is called the nose tackle. In a four-man front, there are two tackles. They line up across from the offensive linemen, on either side of the center.

A defensive tackle's main job is to stop the other team from running the ball. A good offense will try to run the ball straight past the center. This is called running up the middle. When a team tries to run up the middle, the defensive tackles must stop them.

Tackling the running back is not a tackle's only job. Sometimes, the defense needs its tackle(s) to rush the quarterback, too.

A defensive tackle is responsible for stopping running plays in the middle of the field.

FOOTBALL FACT

John Randle of the Minnesota Vikings is a defensive tackle who also likes to rush the quarterback.

Defensive End

A defensive end lines up on either side of the defensive tackle(s). Defensive ends have to be able to tackle running backs. But the main job of an end is to rush the quarterback. Ends are usually quicker than tackles because they have to rush the quarterback. They also have to chase down the running back when he tries to run around the defensive line.

LINEBACKERS

Linebackers line up just behind the defensive line. This starting point gives the linebackers more time to react as the offensive play begins. If a team is playing with four defensive linemen, they usually will have three linebackers. If they are playing three linemen, they play four linebackers.

A linebacker has to be quick and alert.

FOOTBALL: RUSHING AND TACKLING

Linebackers have to be both fast and strong. They have to be fast to cover pass receivers. They also have to be strong enough to tackle ball carriers. At the beginning of each play, the linebackers quickly try to figure out what the offense is doing. If the linebackers see a running play develop, they move toward the ball carrier. If the linebackers see a pass play developing, they try to break up the play. They try to knock down the ball, or they try to cover the receivers.

Sometimes, the linebackers also try to stop the quarterback from passing the ball. On some plays, linebackers will help the defensive linemen rush the passer. When extra players join in the pass rush, this is called a blitz.

Middle Linebacker/Inside Linebackers

Most defenses use one middle linebacker or two inside linebackers. These players have to cover the center of the field. If a running back gets past the defensive tackles, these linebackers have to stop him. If the quarterback tries to pass to a receiver in the middle of the field, these linebackers have to stop the pass.

Defensive backs need to be in great shape.

Outside Linebackers

Outside linebackers usually line up behind the offensive line and away from the middle linebacker. Outside linebackers have to be fast so that they can chase down running backs.

DEFENSIVE BACKS

Defensive backs line up behind the linebackers. These backs often line up deep (far away from the scrimmage line). Defensive backs don't have to be as big as defensive linemen or linebackers. It is more important for them to be fast. Their job is to cover

the receivers. Defensive backs have to keep receivers from catching passes. If a receiver catches a pass, the backs must tackle that receiver. The defensive backs are often the last players on the field who have a chance to tackle the offensive player after a long run or pass. Also, defensive backs sometimes will blitz the quarterback.

There are two types of defensive backs: cornerbacks and safeties.

Cornerbacks

A cornerback's job is to cover the wide receiver. Cornerbacks often are the most athletic players on defense. They have to be quick and agile. They must follow a receiver wherever he goes. They have to stop receivers from getting open and catching passes.

Safeties

Safeties have to be able to cover receivers. They also need to stop the run. Every team has two safeties: a strong safety and a free safety.

Defensive Positions

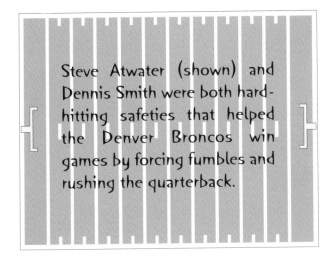

Steve Atwater (shown) and Dennis Smith were both hard-hitting safeties that helped the Denver Broncos win games by forcing fumbles and rushing the quarterback.

• **The strong safety** usually plays on the same side as the offense's tight end. The strong safety must be able to cover the pass and stop the run.

• **The free safety** usually lines up deep and in the center. This position is sometimes called playing centerfield, because the free safety looks like a baseball centerfielder, getting ready to catch a fly ball. But instead of catching baseballs, he is waiting to see what the offense does. He must be ready to tackle the ball carrier if that player gets past the other defenders.

Steve Atwater's outstanding play at the safety position helped the Denver Broncos win Super Bowl XXXII.

TWO

TACKLING

Tackling is the ability to stop the ball carrier by pulling, pushing, or knocking him to the ground. Any contact that makes the ball carrier hit the ground is a good tackle. However, a defender uses some rules to give himself the best chance to make a tackle.

TACKLING FUNDAMENTALS

There are four things to keep in mind when learning how to tackle a player. They are: the angle of pursuit, tackling position, making contact, and desire.

Angle of Pursuit

You don't want to wait for the ball carrier to come to you. If you do, he will gain more yardage for his team. You want to run toward the ball carrier. However, if you run straight at him, he will run to the side and try to get around you. You need to run toward the ball

Tackling is the most important defensive skill.

carrier so that he cannot get past you. The path you take toward the ball carrier is called the angle of pursuit.

Knowing the correct angle of pursuit is a skill learned through drills and practice. To become a good tackler, you have to learn to judge the speed of the ball carrier. This will help you to reach him at the earliest possible moment. It also will help you to stop him from getting around you.

Tackling Position

Developing good tackling skills also means learning the right tackling position. As you approach your target, bend at your knees with your legs spread apart about shoulder width (See Figure 1). This gives you good balance.

Making Contact

As you get close to the ball carrier, take shorter steps. When the moment of contact comes, push off from the foot that is closest to the ball carrier. As you move upward into his body, hit his midsection and chest

Figure 1: Keep your knees bent as you move in for the tackle.

with your shoulder pads. Grab hold of the ball carrier by putting your arms around the player's hips. Try to move the ball carrier up and back. This will stop his forward movement and knock him off balance.

For safety reasons, a tackler should always remember to do two things:

- **Bend from the knees, not from the waist.** Use your leg muscles to drive straight into the player's body.

Tackling

• **Keep your back and your head as close to upright as possible.** Never look down at the ground. If you look down when you make a tackle, you might hit the player with the top of your head. This type of contact could cause serious damage to your head, neck, and back.

Desire

To tackle a player, you need the right level of desire and determination. People have a natural fear of situations in which they could be hurt. Good tacklers know that if they use correct form and stay aggressive, they lessen their chances of getting hurt. They develop a strong mental attitude: "Hit or be hit!"

TACKLING DRILLS

The best way to become a good tackler is to practice tackling drills over and over again. When you first start practicing, start tackling drills that are run at half speed. Then, when you have developed good form, you can run drills at full speed.

Tackling drills help a defense develop good form.

FOOTBALL: RUSHING AND TACKLING

Open-Field Tackling

For a simple tackling drill, practice open-field tackling. Line up ten yards away from a teammate. You are the tackler, and he is the ball carrier. Start by running toward each other. After running for five yards, the ball carrier turns and runs directly left or right. When you see which way the ball carrier is turning, turn, run toward him, and tackle him.

Tackling

Breaking Free

Another good tackling drill is the break-free-and-tackle drill. This drill calls for three players. As the defender, you line up directly across from an offensive blocker. A third player lines up directly behind the offensive lineman. He is the ball carrier.

When the drill begins, the offensive lineman tries to block you. Meanwhile, the ball carrier runs toward the offensive lineman. Try to break free of the offensive lineman by pushing your arms toward his chest. As the running back gets near the offensive lineman, he cuts left or right and continues running up the field. Once you break free from the offensive lineman, go after the running back and tackle him.

THE STUNT

The stunt is a play in which the defense tries to confuse the offense. During a stunt play, two defensive linemen switch their positions when the ball is snapped. Sometimes, the tackles switch places with each other. Other times, a tackle switches places with the defensive end who is lined up next to him. When

A defender must be able to make an open-field tackle.

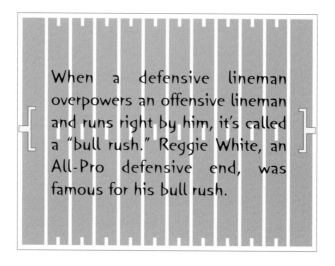

When a defensive lineman overpowers an offensive lineman and runs right by him, it's called a "bull rush." Reggie White, an All-Pro defensive end, was famous for his bull rush.

the football is snapped, one defensive lineman steps in front of the other lineman and tries to rush the passer from that position. The other lineman waits for one second. Then he tries to rush the passer from the other lineman's original position. If the stunt works, a defender may get past the offense line and tackle the ball carrier.

Reggie White (shown right) was one of the NFL's best pass rushers.

RUSHING THE PASSER

Whenever the quarterback drops back to pass, the defense tries to sack him before he throws the ball. This is called rushing the passer. The other team's offensive linemen will do whatever it takes to block the pass rushers. The best pass rushers use their strength and athletic skills to get past the offensive linemen.

PASS-RUSHING SKILLS

Sometimes the pass rusher will be able to run straight at the quarterback. This happens when the offense is confused and the blockers don't know which players to block. More often than not, though, an offensive player will try to block a pass rusher. Developing pass-rushing skills will help the defensive player to get past these blockers and get to the quarterback.

A defensive pass rush can catch the offense by surprise.

Rushing the Passer

The Stance

The first skill you need to develop is the proper stance. The proper stance puts you in position to push forward quickly, without losing balance. Your stance is the same for both running and passing plays. When a tackle or end lines up at the line of scrimmage, he gets into a "three-point stance." In this stance, your feet are spread apart to about the width of your shoulders. Bend at your knees, getting down as low to the ground as possible. Put one hand on the ground to steady your body. Hold your other arm in front of your body, ready for contact with the offensive lineman. Balance your weight on the balls of your feet (See Figure 2). This hunched-over position allows you to drive the blocker up and away from you with a lot of power.

A blitzing linebacker or defensive back sets up in a stance that is very similar to a defensive lineman's stance. He is bent over and his feet are spread. This position protects his body and legs from offensive blockers. However, his hands don't touch the ground.

Figure 2: Pass rushers often use a three-point stance.

Rushing the Passer

The Swim

Throw your arm over the opposite shoulder of the player who is blocking you. Your arm should move just as it would if you were swimming in a pool. Use your arm to push your body over and past the blocker. Once you get past the blocker, you can attack the quarterback.

The Cut

This technique is the opposite of the swim technique. Instead of throwing your arm over the blocker's shoulder, drive your arm below his arm. Once your arm is past the blocker, use your arm to pull the rest of your body past him. At the same time, you push away the blocker.

SENDING THE BLITZ

On most plays, only the defensive linemen try to rush toward the quarterback. But sometimes, linemen have a hard time getting past blockers. Other times, the defense may just want to surprise the quarterback. The blitz is a great way to attack the offense.

A pass rusher must be able to get past the offensive blockers.

FOOTBALL: RUSHING AND TACKLING

When the defense blitzes, they hope to tackle the quarterback behind the line of scrimmage. This is called sacking the quarterback. Even if they don't sack the quarterback, they might make him rush his throw. When the quarterback rushes his throw, he has less of a chance to complete his pass. He might even throw an interception.

The blitz can be a good weapon for the defense. But it is also a risky play. When a player blitzes, he cannot cover the offense's receivers. This gives the receivers a better chance to get open. To stop the quarterback from passing the ball, the blitzers must get to the quarterback as soon as possible.

The blitz can be a powerful weapon for the defense.

FOUR

DEFENSIVE ALIGNMENTS

The defense never knows exactly what play the offense is going to run. However, the defense can guess when it will be a running play or a passing play. To give themselves the best chance to defend against what the offense might run (or throw) at them, the defense chooses an alignment (lineup). The defensive team usually will consist of four linemen, three linebackers, and four defensive backs (two cornerbacks and two safeties). Sometimes the coach may want to change who is on the field during a play, depending on whether he thinks the offense will pass or run.

The most common defensive alignments include the 4-3 defense, the 3-4 defense, the nickel defense, and the dime defense.

The defense will use different
formations depending on game situations.

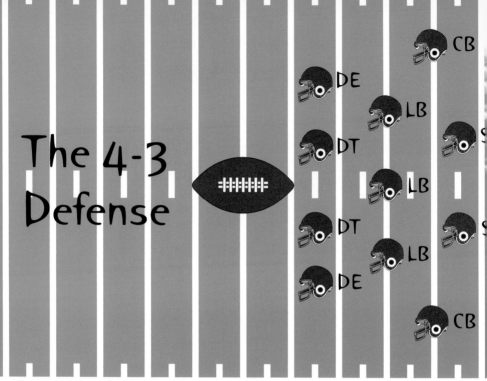

Figure 3 (above): The 4-3 defense is a commonly used formation.
Figure 4 (below): The 3-4 defense has three linemen and four linebackers.

Defensive Alignments

The 4-3 Defense

For a 4-3 defense, the team puts four defensive linemen (two tackles and two ends) on the line of scrimmage. There are three linebackers and four defensive backs (two cornerbacks and two safeties) (See Figure 3). Many teams use a 4-3 defense as their main defensive alignment.

The 3-4 Defense

Some teams use the 3-4 defense as their main alignment. The 3-4 uses three linemen and four linebackers (See Figure 4). In this alignment, the coach is sacrificing the strength and size of a lineman for the speed of a linebacker. If a coach has a lot of good linebackers, he may want to run a 3-4 defense.

The Nickel Defense

This defensive alignment is similar to a 4-3 defense or a 3-4 defense. The one difference is that one of the linebackers is replaced with an extra defensive back (See Figure 5). That puts five defensive backs on the field. This is where the name "nickel defense" comes

from (five backs on the field, five cents in a nickel). The extra back is called the "nickel back."

Teams go to the nickel defense when it seems likely that the offense will try to pass the ball. The extra defensive back may help to cover a receiver. He also may help blitz the quarterback.

The Dime Defense

The dime defense uses one linebacker and six defensive backs (See Figure 6). A coach or a defensive coordinator will use the dime defense only when he is absolutely sure that the offense will pass the ball. The extra defensive backs make it harder for receivers to get open and catch a pass.

They say the best defense is a good offense, but a good defense helps a team's offense. When a team's defense keeps the other team from scoring, the offense will not have to score as many points to win the game. If you follow the proper techniques for tackling and pass-rushing, you can become part of a great defense.

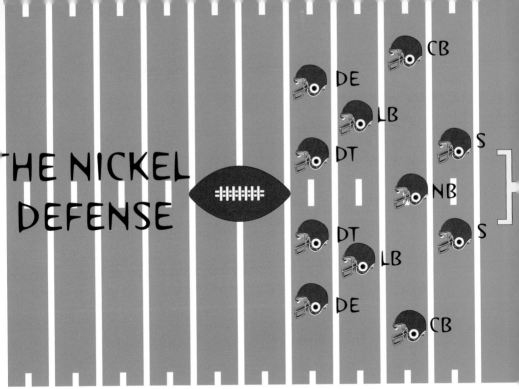

Figure 5 (above): The nickel defense adds a "nickel back" (NB).
Figure 6 (below): The dime defense adds two defensive backs (DBs).

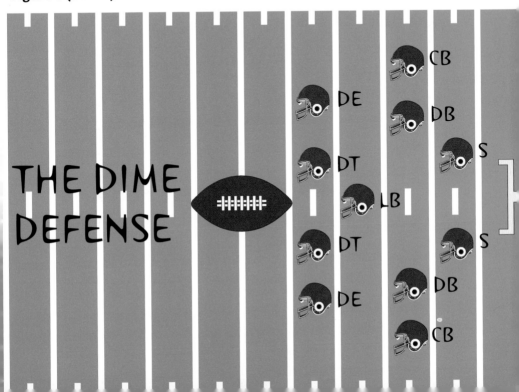

NEW WORDS

alignment a team's lineup

angle of pursuit the direction in which a defensive player runs to tackle the ball carrier

blitz when the defense tries to surprise the offense by sending extra pass rushers

deep far past the line of scrimmage

defensive backfield the cornerbacks and safeties who cover pass plays

defensive linemen the defensive ends and defensive tackles on the scrimmage line

dime defense when the defense sends off two linebackers and replaces them with two extra defensive backs

linebackers the defensive players who cover the
middle of the field

line of scrimmage the spot on the field that
marks the beginning of the play

nickel back an extra defensive back added in
the nickel defense

nickel defense when the defense sends off a
linebacker and replaces him with an extra
defense back

pass rush when the defense tries to sack the
quarterback

sack when the defense tackles the quarterback
behind the line of scrimmage

FOR FURTHER READING

Allen James. *Football: Play Like a Pro*. Mahwah, N.J.: Troll Communications L.L.C., 1990.

Bass, Tom. *Play Football the NFL Way*. New York: St. Martin's Griffin, 1991.

Buckley, James Jr. *Football*. New York: D.K. Publishing, Incorporated, 1999.

Christopher, Matt. *Fighting Tackle*. New York: Little, Brown, & Company, 1996.

Morgan, Terri and Stew Thornley. *Junior Seau High-Voltage Linebacker*. Minneapolis, MN: The Lerner Publishing Group, 1996.

RESOURCES

ESPN: Canadian Football League (CFL)

http://espn.go.com/cfl

This is ESPN's Web page on the Canadian Football League (CFL).

Football Drills

www.footballdrills.com

Learn drills to practice every football position, including tackling and pass rushing drills.

The National Football League

www.nfl.com

Learn about your favorite NFL defensive players. Get statistics and read interviews with the players.

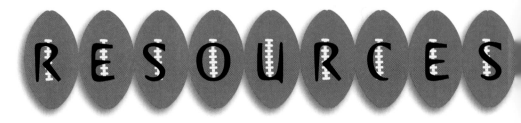

Pop Warner Football

www.tdclub.com/ysnim/home/index.jsp

This online center contains information about Pop Warner, the youth football league. It also has links to games, comics, and news about football.

INDEX

INDEX

ABOUT THE AUTHOR

Stephen Holden is a avid, lifelong football fan. Steve learned his love of football from his father, who was a star high school and college football player. Steve's favorite teams are the Syracuse Orangemen and the New York Giants. His all-time favorite defensive player is Lawrence Taylor.